OCEAN MOODS

OCEAN MOODS

Dave Grieve

First published 2012
by Mudfog Press
c/o Arts and Events, Culture and Tourism,
P.O. Box 99A, Civic Centre, Middlesbrough, TS1 2QQ
www.mudfog.co.uk

Cover Design by turnbull.fineart@btinternet.com

Print by EPW Print & Design Ltd.

ISBN: 978-1-8995039-3-6

Mudfog Press gratefully acknowledges
the support of Arts Council England.

Acknowledgements

My thanks to Andy Willoughby and Bob Beagrie for
directing me onto the edifying road to writing poetry.
Also, a very special thanks to S. J. Litherland for her
patient, professional and priceless guidance as my
Mentor. Thanks to Alan Turnbull for the excellent
cover design. My thanks also to Tom Richardson for
his editorial advice and to all the help and guidance
received from the volunteers that give up their spare
time to work at the Mudfog Press. Thanks also to my
good wife Jeanette for her encouragement and
patience.

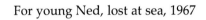
For young Ned, lost at sea, 1967

Contents

Ocean Moods

Is the sea in my heart? In my tainted soul?
Yes and yes. I feel the Ocean
constant within, even at my rest.

Did Poseidon and Neptune battle
for her favours? If so, who was
the victor? I often ponder this.

I venture neither: not myth
nor being embraced all she needs;
no painted whore, she will give

freely of her body to sailors,
sanctions honest, heroic mariners
a good bounty.

I ply her, she tries my mettle
to the bounds. I venerate her;
I fear her callous rage.

She fears only my detritus.
She despises delinquent ways
that harm her be-jewelled realm.

Provoked, she will vent her wrath:
her allies are mighty. The great God Thor
will raise the cardinal winds to gales.

She may call Anemoi, Auster, Kon,
Quebu: potent Gods of tempest winds.
Great, black, lightning-ripped clouds

will engulf vessels and hearts.
Her wild charge will take up then guzzle
useless men and flotsam.

When Khonsu, the silver night traveller,
casts his brilliant cloak, her pristine shores
become shadowed mystery.

She will show small mercy and cast up
chosen messengers. They will tell
of her scaly backed rage.

Young Ned

Young Ned is missing.
We searched stem to stern,
found not sight nor sign.

He's alone in the ocean,
afraid. Calls unheeded.

How deep the Indian is.
He'll fall through layers
of warm and cold;

Poseidon may claim
his sea smitten soul.

Did he love? Was he loved?
Only mess-mates know.

The belly of multitudes
of the ocean's denizens
will be his nomadic grave.

I'll record his proven life
as white as his bones.
He'll travel well to his God.

Only my eyes knew Ned:
red hair, freckles:
great strength, able.
A bright, willing hand.

Silent forlorn search closes.
Course is set South-Westerly.

Night Fire

St Elmo came at two bells, first watch,
pointing his torch, igniting our rigging
lightning blue.

The shimmering aura duped my eyes.
That electric tingle crawled upon flesh,
bristled hair.

Awe etched in weathered features.
Some smiled, then brows furrowed,
unease.

Low *whished* murmurs hushed.
Dripping humidity forced gnarly hands
to wipe brows.

St Elmo inspired, dredging
primordial senses;

I have witnessed famed Aurora Borealis,
I've stepped back from floating
blue-white plasma.

Only the light of the mariners' saint
stirred deep my inner spirit.

That Bastard Storm

In the easterly force ten gale,
sixty hours pounded by that storm;

a half mile off our starboard beam
Simonstown's boozers beckoned.

Incessant raging sea tested
short-fused frigate's crew.

Moon raking giants capped
with furious spume loomed over.

A constant, un-nerving racket as
bulk-heads and deck-heads to keel

protested loudly at ocean's malice.

'Tween decks was awash,
slopped food in abundance.

Galley pots and crocks clattered
and skittered about.

In the heads, plumes of bog water.

My stint as lifebuoy ghost done,
I welcomed my relief. He was able.

The after wash-deck was perilous.
Stinging spindrift raced the wind.

Could I get safe below? Avoiding
barked shins I made it. Old salt.

Not of a faith, I wished with a will:
respite, that bastard storm gone and

peace aboard our battered home.

The Young Officer's Voice

I was sitting aft on the quarter deck
drinking bad coffee, smoking, alone;
a whispered voice carried by a wraith
came from the West upon a breeze.

HMS Phoebe in the Gulf of Aden,
passing by Socotra and into the Indian.
It was the voice of a young officer of
the RFAS Apple Leaf.

I had met him some days before
whilst standing guard aboard the Leaf,
at buoys off Steamer Point, watching
for insurgents floating with debris
to clamp a mine onto the hull.

He'd stopped for a chat, didn't want
to be there: who did? I felt his fear;

I don't know how I knew it was his voice.
The whispering voice uttered but one word: *'Davy'*

The whole crew were roused and
stood to: A man had gone missing off
the RFA, she'd put to sea hours after us.

The missing soul was a young lieutenant:
I wondered: could it have been the
unhappy officer who confided in me?
Maybe he surrendered to his fear.

Did he call me
with his ultimate breath?
If so I was honoured,
but sad there was none other.

Marching to the Prize-Giving

Marching inland, the tiny harbour
behind us. Mixed odours
of the Red Sea, the fish-market
and wasted bodies of the near dead,
the name of their Messiah,

Haile Selassie, upon their lips.
Bony fingers tugged at trousers.
They pleaded: mumbled prayers
over sick infants amidst flies.

'EYES FRONT!' We march out of step,
avoiding prone bodies. Icy cold
fingers touched mine, I recoiled.
'Steady lads,' the Lieutenant's voice
quivered. Smothered sobs

gagged rugged Sailors front and rear.
An iron fist gripped my gut, reached
to my throat: I felt stinging tears
coursing weathered features.

Our pace quickened, we marched on.
We wanted to run.

'Do not attempt to help these people,'
was the standing order.
'WHY?' screamed my brain, breaking
my heart. *'We cannot help them all.',*
was harsh reality. We marched on.

It would be remiss of us to be late
for the prize-giving!

Out of sight and earshot, a small Man
in Naval uniform gazes into bleary eyes.
His blue serge festooned with sparkling
medals. Well fed, well dressed;

devotees applauded. His toothy grin
almost out-shone the state limousine.
Could he not smell his people dying?
Was he deaf to his revered name upon

their trembling lips?

Arabian Walls

Aden, a lifetime ago

I have touched warm Arabian walls.
Have felt the hot snap of copper-coats.
My mouth was dry. Adrenalin rushed.
Fear overtook and dominated every sense.

My fingers played in deep, burnt holes.
My ears sang with the sound of gunfire.
My nose stung with the stink of cordite.
I baulked at the stench of decomposition.

Flies gorged on dark, congealing blood.
Lifeless eyes stared into fanatical afterlife.
I thank nobody or nothing for my life.
I grieve heartfelt for those innocent dead.

Mombasa

I had a nap inside an
Elephant's tusk in
Kilindini district;

I awoke amidst the
clamour of a market.

Black men and women
with shiny faces and
dazzling teeth beamed:

I bought a Rhino
and a Giraffe;

I drank more Tusker
beer. I returned to that
tusk and slept well.

My animals dried
out and cracked.

I buried them at sea.
Unlike warm African
recollections, they

drifted away on
silent, rolling waves.

Towards Cook Island

The sturdy Barque is driven
hard before following seas:
she grapples with notorious

gales, the Roaring Forties.
Spindrift rises and dances
across plunging forepeak.

Glittering globules fly madly
about in gusting, cyclonic
winds laying rugs of sparkling

salt upon holystoned decks
pitching and rolling underfoot
in lee of weathered bulwarks.

Refracted rays make rainbow
awnings that quickly vanish:
then more prismatic magic.

Agile sailors scramble aloft to
reduce sail further, weathered,
calloused hands cling white-

knuckled to swaying shrouds.
Flying fish burst from rolling
blue-grey crags twixt peak

and trough: silvery scales
flash in brumes of briny.
Flicking caudal fins leave

patterns of eddies that quickly
merge with the entire majesty
of wild ocean nature.

Hold hard the taffrail boy. Hold
hard, or she'll certain take you.
She will garnish her fathomless
garden with your flensed bones.

The Dutchman's Prize

The phantom hulk emerged
silent from rolling fogbank
a fathom and-a-half above
swelling sea. Her wretched,
wraith-like crew turned to
in ominous quietude tending
dripping, kelp hung ropes,
rigging and ragged canvas
reefed upon shadowy yards,
masts and blackened shrouds.

The spectre veers inexorably to starboard.

The Flying Dutchman bore
down upon hapless Coble.
The single lateen spar
frantically hauled to top,
canvas stretched taut:

Too late, too slow, the fearful
apparition claims her prize.

Thoughts of Home

After a wearying watch,
I would think of home
until sleep. Apart from ship

and Pompey, where was home?
Middlesbrough is adopted.
Will she ever accept me?

Yezdech led me here,
nigh fifty years ago.
Bless big Al Yezdech.

Eye-opening leap for a
Londoner. The old town
appeared darkly menacing,

strange odours, dull hues,
nice smiles, hard looks.

I'd never seen a blast-furnace:

a dull roar, plumes
of orange and red fire,
showers of yellow sparks,
bathed the scene in blazing light
and dancing shadows:

I was taken aback.
Yezdech nudged me:
"They're casting."

The evening sky over
Grangetown, playing host
to swaying, snaking, purple
polluting fire devils: "Flare-stacks,"
murmured Yezdech.

Gritty, forthright town,
gritty, forthright people.

Knights of Steel

Three smoky, steaming crags crowd the Teesside sky-
line.
Clay Lane's blast furnaces stand upon black ground,
making steel.

The folks of South Bank cough up dusty fall-out of
furnaces.
They do not complain, their livelihood depends upon
making steel.

To put food on table, a roof over the heads of chesty
kids, robust wives;
week by week, shift by shift, willing men toil
doggedly making steel.

Fitters, Welders, Burners, Riggers, Skilled and Semi-
skilled Tradesmen,
delegated, dedicated to install and maintain
equipment for making steel.

On cast house floor, rawhide clad knights of steel
ready for sweet pints,
get grimy, gritty. Prepared for the smoking heat of
Hades, making steel.

A siren screams the imminent tapping of the furnace's
molten yield.
A shielded knight assails the clay plug. A dicey
process, making steel.

His visor reflects the task, he stabs, drives home a
Blazing oxylance.
The crumbling clay yields, liberating a river of Hell.
He's making steel.

More knights take station at the edge of streams of boiling metal.
Flames reach to burn, vicious sparks fly at the stalwarts making steel.

The knights coax the sparkling melt with heavy bars and flat-rakes.
A sand barrier keeps searing heat at bay, a trade-trick, making steel.

The cast makes its smouldering way to cascade into brick-lined vessel.
Plumes of acrid smoke and fire fill Hellish ether.
Polluting, making steel.

Hundreds of tons of slow-cooling steel ready for processing at the mills.
Enriching Britain, Earth and its people. It's rewarding making steel.

Sweating knights retire to cabin to quaff mugs of tea and munch crusty butties.
Soon, another cast, they'll resume making steel.

Shift over: a pint of Bass in 'Mucky Pots' for weary, soap-smelling men
away home to a good tea. They'll reflect upon the tough shift, making steel.

A hard eight hours ahead for those filing in to clock on for the next shift.
Another group of workers ready for the inexorable cycle, of making steel.

The Cheap Cider Path

I would surface slowly
from the stupor; I became
the soiled ground,

the cheap cider path
made by useless wasters
like me: Dead-beats.

The way becomes blurred:
has no substance,
no direction,

meanders from life
toward yearned death.

The poison elevates ego:
You're wonderful,
clever, smooth.

Sinking noble pasts,
replaces dignity
with sloth and slobbery.

'The stale piss of Satan!'
If a man can't drink hard,
fight hard, he isn't a man.

Big Eric drank and sank.
Cheap cider the killer.
Certain death for less

than a quid a bottle.
Once a big man. Ex-RAF.
Once a family man.

I saw his ghost walking: I
saw mine walking with it.

A long suffering,
exasperated lady
took reign and set

about the daunting
task of righting her
wayward man.
She browbeat, nagged
and nurtured. It aged her.
She cursed my existence.

Sorry for me, sorry for knowing me.
Regretting, loving and caring.

I apologise to the world
for wasting its time.

I thank my wife for my life.

Lost

In a dark corner of a dark alley
upon damp cobbles lies a wretched
creature: I note a shoe-less foot
quivering and can hear whimpers

uttered from the wet foetal shape;
he has shunned aid and charity:
his every fibre craves more poison.

Was this ever a man lying here?

Old salts will know of his time,
they will recall his great strength,
his tenacious courage in adversity.
Dispatches proudly record him.

His pawned medals boast silver bars.

What dark tragedy laid him thus?
Perhaps betrayal, lost love or friend?
I stare, pondering self-consciously.

I thank the renowned stars of fortune,
here, but for human charity, go I!

Walls

Walls in this place whisper of souls
struggling to remain in wasted hosts
within this asylum, wherein sanity

long since lost its way. My once
rebellious spirit cowers. Am I
hearing voices from perdition?

Am I required in that infernal place?
The wards smell of stale piss, shit,
and vomit. A malodorous blanket

envelops me. My eyes and nose sting,
secrete an emulsion of tears and blood.
A harsh, canvas bolster rubs raw my face,

dragging my filthy, matted hair.
My wrists and ankles are sorely fettered.
Thick leather straps cut across my chest.

They grow tighter when I struggle and
the pains in my guts are exquisite.
This is my Hell. It is of my making,

brought by powdery white lines of nowhere
and poisonous concoctions of dark illusion.

Cells

It's difficult to love at arm's length:
impossible.

I learned this protesting violently
in a cold cell.

Pained, frustrated, humiliated:
I learned.

It's agony seeing my kids
grow away.

Harrowing describes my sense
of abandonment.

On comprehension of fearful errors
I rage inwardly.

Neither tears nor blood lift the dark
cowl of shame;

I conceive of no crossroad,
no illuminated tunnel.

To recover, to return seems unlikely.
Courage, a stranger.

Canal Walk

Stroll along the canal tow-path
from Brentford to Southall.

Each footfall touches old lives.

Tread upon shoe-worn ground,
shoes of horses and men alike;

men that have aged with horses
and trod countless steps as one.

Look about you. Please city eyes,
inhale deeply, purge city air.

Listen to sighs of soft breezes
and gentle rustling of leaves.

Smell perfumes of wild flowers.
Taste fruits no longer enjoyed.

Touch the bark of an Alder
feel its benevolent knowledge.

Bow to its noble existence.

Observe decaying lock-gates;
look into the muddy water.

See the reflection of mortality;
gaze into the murky depths.

Watch for any movement.
You may glimpse the spectre

of a boy I knew. He drowned.
There, his favourite playground.

Bad Day in Chiswick

I was four or five
when I saw
Jimmy Lee getting
beaten with nailed
wood. Big boys.

His tears ran silent as
his blood.

Also that day
the window cleaner
fell off his ladder.
He broke something.
Maybe everything.
He twitched awhile,
then was still.

The water ran out of
his bucket.

Soldiers

My six man army stood motionless.
Looked awkward on the clipped mat.

I was proud. They were magnificent in
scarlet tunics and plumed bear skins.

I hefted each individual guard,
I relished their tactile heaviness.

They were standing at attention, rifles
at the slope. One or two bayonets bent.

Father's steps were uneven on the stairs.

Mother led me to my sister's room.
Margaret hugged me, we felt each other's fear.

The argument raged. Ugly, frightening.

We stepped quietly into the kitchen.
Father was snoring loudly in the front room.

Mother sobbed soulfully, head in hands.
I returned to my soldiers, tears blurring my eyes.

My little army had been crushed.
I stared at the twisted, flattened remains.

In the debris I saw my Father's body.

Aunt Kit's Dark Room

Mother took me there. The room
was dark, the gloom had weight.
There was a black cat. It was fat.
It stared balefully without blinking.

Ominous tick tick of the mantle clock.

The walls and ceilings were brown,
the mouldings stained. The room stunk
of fag smoke, air muggy with the fug.

Ominous tick tick of the mantle clock.

Blackout curtains hung heavily.
A spear of street light pierced
the smoky gloom, stark, dust-speckled.
The dark furniture stood solidly.

The coal fire was just alive.

Ominous tick tick of the mantle clock.

Mother, Aunt Anne and Aunt Kit
and Joan were hunched, murmuring.
Aunt Kit's voice rose, taut, strangled.
She wept. The sisters rallied and hugged.

Ominous tick tick of the mantle clock.

My eyelids felt gritty on my eyeballs.
Dark, then not so dark, then darkest.
I sank deep inside the clammy darkness.
The big pale man lay in the heavy bed.

Ominous tick tick of the mantle clock.

He was cold and still.

Laundry Day

Abundant steam, smelly carbolic,
boiling water. The whole kitchen
a steamy cocoon; I was the pupa.

Mum's bright, flowery turban, her face
and hands scarlet, damp fading pinny.
She hums to tunes on *Workers Playtime*.

Scalding pans bubbling away. Pristine
sheets, pillow cases, vests and shirts.
Sinewy arms and elegant hands fed

a sheet corner into the mangle. Soon
the sheet lay dead in the old tin bath.
Dresses, blouses, drawers and socks

were next to fall; no quarter given.
A bob for the gas meter. Flannels
and towels next into gaping copper.

More grated soap, a cup of soda, a wipe
of the moist brow. More steamy washing
to be fettled. I gaze about the kitchen cloud.

Something good settles inside me.

We relish warm sweet tea. Mum smiles
and all is well. The world is perfect
within my spotless, steamy haven.

Ageing

My tired, clouded, ageing mind
no longer has the gift of clear memory,
nor my rheumy eyes sharp certainty,
nor my hearing sweet clarity.

My muscles are soft and flabby,
my bones tend easily to break;
lethargy rules my every action
as strong medication dictates.

Arteries harden as walls grow thick,
joints move with an audible click.

Old age, my friend, inexorable old age:
it will transpire sooner than you think:
your hair will thin as will your skin.
Crows feet where you grin and wink.

Don't fret my friend. It's pleasant on a Sunday
when grandchildren visit and stay 'till Monday.

Welcome the Moon

Privet: dull green leaves.
Old tree: dampened, grey and black.
Winter: blackbirds, worms.

Shed quivers in wind.

Is that snow I see?
Flakes falling slowly, sparsely.
So comely, so cold.

A welcome full moon.

Friend or Foe

I have known all her moods.

Warm, frigid, friendly, angry.
I have never trusted her,
though I have loved her;
about her, in her; upon

her many shores.

She has been my livelihood.
She has cost me much: often
she has tried to best me, often
she has tried to take me to

her lovely, deadly depths.

The Ocean was my mistress.
At times she possessed me.
On occasion, I owned her.
We lived, loved and fought

nigh a lifetime;

I miss her. Or do I?

Some Navy Speak

Matelot: Royal Navy Rating, Able Seaman
Lamp Tramp: unskilled Ships Electrician
Boot Neck: Royal Marine
Sparks. Signals Rating, radio
Pipe: on board signal using Bosun's Call - type of whistle
Rum Bosun: collects, measures and issues rum to grog members of individual mess-decks
Grog members/Rum rats: Ratings over the age of 20 who draw daily rum ration
Pussers: anything supplied by the R.N.
Jack Dusty: Leading Stores rating
Queens: extra rum (spillage).
Copper. copper measuring vessel
Rum Fanny: two gallon square bucket, the inside of which is never touched (*virginal*)
Dab-toe: naval rating, Seaman branch
Make and mend: free afternoon
Tropical Routine: working day, Middle and Far East Fleet. 0600-1300 hrs except watchkeepers
Uckers: board game akin to Ludo
Ogin: the Ocean
Goffer: large wave or sweet drink/hair style
Baby's Head: steak and kidney pudding
Pot Mess: stew made from everything served from huge cauldron. Rough sea
Bung-Hole: cheese
Figgy duff: pudding
Spam Javelins/pork swords: sausages
Slide: butter/margarine
Malta Dog: diarrhoea.
Rabbit: gift
Rabbit Run: shopping trip for Rabbits
Party: girl/woman.
Gronk: plain looking, homely girl/woman
Doggo: ugly man

Sippers, Gulpers, half tot, full tot: Measures of rum for bartering or repayment of favour. (Full tot = one third of pint: 3 part water, 1 part rum, 100 per-cent proof. Measure issued neat when in action.)

Biography

Dave Grieve was born in Hammersmith, London. He left secondary school aged 15 without qualifications. He drifted from job to job until aged 18 whereupon he joined the Royal Navy. He took up residence in the Middlesbrough area after a brief visit in 1968 and decided to make the Boro his home. He remained in the RN until 1974, worked for a brief period in the steel industry. However, having 'itchy feet,' as it were, he gained a Board Of Trade Certificate and went back to sea in the Merchant Navy. After a spell of service in the MN, he gained employment with a Dutch dredging company and worked on contracts in England and Scotland. He has also worked on demolition and construction projects throughout the UK. Unfortunately, Dave was forced into early retirement by serious illness.

He first became interested in writing whilst serving in the RN, but did not have the opportunity to write seriously until he retired. He attended two Creative Writing courses under the auspices of Bob Beagrie and Andy Willoughby. Their influence led him on to the path of writing Poetry. He has had poems published in the anthologies, The Eye Of Temenos, Museum Of My Life and the magazine Kenaz. He has also self published a collection of short stories, Four Little Gems, the proceeds of which he gave to various local charities.

Dave's other hobbies include wood sculpture/carving, and abstract painting.